DISCARD  W9-BSJ-052

PRINCE HARRY & MEGHAN

PRINCE HARRY & MEGHAN

Royals for a New Era

JILL SHERMAN

LERNER PUBLICATIONS ◆ MINNEAPOLIS

Lerner Publications Company
A division of Lerner Publishing Group, Inc.
241 First Avenue North
Minneapolis, MN USA 55401

For reading levels and more information, look up this title at www.lernerbooks.com.

Image credits: BEN STANSALL/AFP/Getty Images, p. 2; Max Mumby/Indigo/Getty Images, p. 6; Dominic Lipinski/PA Images/Getty Images, p. 8; Mirrorpix/Getty Images, p. 9; Victoria Jones/WPA Pool/Getty Images, p. 10; Tim Graham/Getty Images, pp. 11, 12; Martin Keene/PA Images/Getty Images, p. 13; Jayne Fincher/Princess Diana Archive/Getty Images, p. 14; PIERRE BOUSSEL/AFP/Getty Images, p. 16; JEFF J. MITCHELL/AFP/Getty Images, p. 17; Antony Jones/UK Press/Getty Images, p. 19; John Stillwell/PA Images/Getty Images, p. 21; Pool/Anwar Hussein Collection/Getty Images, p. 22; JOHN STILLWELL/AFP/Getty Images, p. 23; CARL DE SOUZA/AFP/Getty Images, p. 24; John Stillwell/WPA Pool/Getty Images, p. 26; Samir Hussein/WireImage/Getty Images, pp. 27, 28, 30; Trae Patton/NBC/Getty Images, p. 33; AF archive/Alamy Stock Photo, p. 34; Danny Lawson/PA Images/Getty Images, p. 37; ANDREW MATTHEWS/AFP/Getty Images, p. 39 (middle); OLI SCARFF/AFP/Getty Images, p. 39 (upper right); Danny Lawson/WPA Pool/Getty Images, p. 40; Paul Ellis/PA Images/Getty Images, p. 41.

Cover: Max Mumby/Indigo/Getty Images.

Main body text set in Rotis Serif Std 55 Regular 13.5/17.
Typeface provided by Adobe Systems.

Library of Congress Cataloging-in-Publication Data

The Cataloging-in-Publication Data for *Prince Harry & Meghan: Royals for a New Era* is on file at the Library of Congress.
ISBN 978-1-5415-3945-7 (lib. bdg.)
ISBN 978-1-5415-3946-4 (eb pdf)

Manufactured in the United States of America
1-45178-36079-5/24/2018

CONTENTS

Prince Harry and Meghan Markle appear together in the Sunken Garden at Kensington Palace after news of their engagement became public. The couple posed for photographs and spoke with reporters.

Prince Harry of Wales and Meghan Markle beamed at each other. While cameras flashed and reporters buzzed around them, they stood comfortably, arm in arm. The two were on the front steps of Kensington Palace, the home of the British royal family in London, England. Harry was wearing a fitted blue suit, and Meghan was in a white trench coat. But the photographers had their eyes on something else: Meghan's diamond engagement ring.

After dating for a little more than a year, Harry and Meghan became engaged. They officially announced the engagement on November 27, 2017. Harry had designed the engagement ring. The ring's stones held great sentimental value for him. The center stone came from Botswana, an African country Harry visited with Meghan when they first started dating. The two outer stones belonged to his famous mother, Diana, Princess of Wales. Harry included those stones to honor his mother and, as he put it, "to make sure that she's with us on this crazy journey together."

Meghan's ring sparkles as she wears it publicly for the first time at Kensington Palace.

The announcement took the United Kingdom and the rest of the world by storm. The British royal family has always been fascinating to the public, and the prospect of a royal wedding was hugely exciting. The news that Meghan would join the royal family was especially interesting to people in the United States. It was once traditional for members of the royal family to marry other members of the British aristocracy. But Meghan is no aristocrat. She is not even British. Meghan is an American.

But despite being something of an outsider, she has been welcomed warmly into the royal family. People around the world followed the wedding closely and watched as Harry and Meghan formed a new royal family.

Born a Royal

Prince Henry Charles Albert David was born on September 15, 1984, in London. Everyone calls him Harry.

Harry is the second child of Charles and Diana, Prince and Princess of Wales. Harry's older brother, William, was born in 1982. And his grandmother is Elizabeth II, the queen of the United Kingdom. Harry's full title is His Royal Highness Prince Henry of Wales. As the grandson of the queen, he is sixth in line for the throne. So Harry probably will never become the king.

Charles and Diana, the Prince and Princess of Wales, leave the hospital with baby Harry in September 1984.

The British Monarchy

The monarchy is the oldest form of government in the United Kingdom, which includes the countries of England, Scotland, Wales, and Northern Ireland. At one time, the king or queen ruled these nations by making laws. These days, the United Kingdom is a constitutional monarchy in which the king or queen is the chief representative of the country but cannot make laws. Parliament is the legislative branch that writes and passes laws.

Queen Elizabeth II is the current British monarch.

The British monarch remains the head of state for sixteen nations known as the Commonwealth Realms. These include Antigua and Barbuda, Australia, the Bahamas, Barbados, Belize, Canada, Grenada, Jamaica, New Zealand, Papua New Guinea, Solomon Islands, St. Christopher and Nevis, St. Lucia, St. Vincent and the Grenadines, Tuvalu, and the United Kingdom.

The monarch is also the head of the Church of England. Members of the royal family use their position to bring attention to important issues. They also can play a role in diplomacy (keeping peace between different countries) by meeting with leaders of foreign nations.

Harry (*right*) and William play at a piano while Diana looks on just a few weeks after Harry's first birthday.

Growing up in the spotlight wasn't always easy. But Harry's mother, Diana, did her best to make sure her children had normal childhood experiences. She kept William and Harry away from the press. And she tried to show them what life was like outside of royal palaces and estates. She took them on the bus and the tube (subway system) in London, and then they would shop at Marks and Spencer, a British department store, and eat at McDonald's. They played in public parks and took normal vacations. The family went to beaches, water parks and, on one occasion, Disney World. But as members of the royal family, they also had a duty to visit foreign countries and attend official events. Harry was only eight months old when he took his first overseas tour. He and his family visited Italy, where cheering crowds came to see the growing royal family.

In contrast to their royal lives, Diana exposed William and Harry to the difficulties that many people experienced. She showed them that it was important to help people who were less fortunate. Diana took her boys to homeless shelters and hospitals. She wanted to show William and Harry that all people mattered, and that a healthy society needed to care for everyone. Diana often spent time talking with people in need, and her work drew attention to important problems. Diana was dedicated to helping others, and she made sure that her boys understood that they could help too.

The family spent their weekdays in London at Kensington Palace and their weekends at Highgrove House, the royal estate near Gloucestershire. There, Harry could spend time outdoors and enjoy the country. He loved animals and had a lop-eared rabbit, which he kept in a hutch in the

Diana and her sons enjoy the fresh air at Highgrove House in the countryside west of London.

Harry (*second from left*) arrives for his first day at Ludgrove School.

stables there. He also spent hours feeding and attending to the sheep on the estate.

When Harry was old enough, he went to his first private school. At the age of three, he began attending Mrs. Mynors' Nursery School. At first, little Harry was too shy to speak to his teachers. Harry's fun-loving spirit soon became apparent, however.

In 1989 Harry started going to the Wetherby School in London, where his brother, William, was already a student. At seven years old, Harry again followed his brother, this time to Ludgrove School in Berkshire. Though he was not a great student, he excelled at sports and other after-school activities. Ludgrove offered a wide

Harry (*right*) rides a ski lift with his mother and brother in Austria in 1991. Harry still enjoys skiing.

range of sports. Harry excelled at cricket, soccer, rugby, and tennis.

He made a couple of close friends at school, including Henry van Straubenzee. The two visited each other on holidays and spent vacations together. Harry went with Henry's family every year to a rental house in North Cornwall. They ate barbecue and ice cream. They explored the sandy beaches, caught shrimp, and went surfing. Later in the summer, Henry would stay with Harry at Kensington Palace. Diana would take the boys to watch the Royal Tournament, a military demonstration. Thousands of members of the military attended. Tanks, guns, and motorbikes were on display. These demonstrations sparked Harry's fascination with the military.

A National Tragedy

In 1996 Charles and Diana announced their divorce. The news did not come as a surprise. They had been having problems in their marriage for some time, and the couple had separated a few years earlier. Their divorce became a scandal that was in the news daily, and Harry had difficulty escaping the gossip. Paparazzi aggressively followed and photographed the family wherever they went.

In August 1997, William and Harry were vacationing with their father in Balmoral, Scotland. The boys had just returned from a trip to southern France with their mother. After the vacation, Diana traveled to Paris. In the early hours of August 31, Diana died in a car crash in that city. When William and Harry, who were just fifteen and twelve years old, woke up later that morning, Charles delivered the terrible news.

Harry and William were devastated. Later that day, Charles took his sons to church so that they could reflect on their mother's death. The family stayed in Scotland to grieve privately during the funeral arrangements.

Meanwhile, rumors spiraled about the cause of the crash. Paparazzi were following Diana's car, hoping to capture a picture of the former princess. Diana; her romantic partner, Dodi Al-Fayed; and the driver died in the crash. After an investigation, the driver was blamed for the accident. However, the driver had been trying to lose the paparazzi following them. Harry, already annoyed by the photographers who followed him daily, became even more resentful of the constant cameras.

The car Diana traveled in was going well above the speed limit when it crashed.

The United Kingdom was in mourning. People around the world loved Diana. They remembered her as incredibly warm, kind, and generous. Her death at the age of thirty-six was tragic. Diana's funeral aired on televisions across the world. Billions of people tuned in to watch and mourn her death. One of the most touching images was of the funeral procession. William and Harry, along with other relatives, walked behind her casket. A horse-drawn carriage carried Diana to her final resting place in Althorp Estate, Diana's family home in Northampton.

Charles kept William and Harry out of the public eye after the funeral. Harry had nightmares about his mother's death and struggled to cope with it. Charles decided to bring Harry with him on an official tour to

Africa in late October. Diana had recently been to Africa and had hoped that her sons would one day go there. While he was there, Harry went to Botswana and also visited a Zulu village.

Though he has a hard time talking about his mother, Harry misses her and thinks of her daily. "Every day, depending on what I'm doing, I wonder what it would be like if she was here, and what she would say, and how

Harry (*second from right*) walks in the procession at his mother's funeral. About 2.5 billion people around the world watched the funeral on television.

she would be making everybody else laugh," he reflected. "Who knows what the situation would be, what the world would be like, if she were still around."

Asking for Help

Harry was just twelve years old when his mother died. As a member of the royal family, he tried not to show his emotions in public. To cope, Harry tried to shut down his emotions entirely. "My way of dealing with it was sticking my head in the sand, refusing to ever think about my mom, because why would that help, it's only going to make you sad, it's not going to bring her back," he said.

When Harry was in his late twenties, he began to realize that not talking about his mother's death was hurting him. His brother urged him to seek therapy to help him deal with his grief and emotions.

Therapy made a big difference in Harry's life. He noted, "There's huge merit in talking about your issues. . . . Keeping it quiet . . . [is] only ever going to make it worse. Not just for you, but for everyone else around you as well, because you become a problem." That's why Harry, along with his brother and sister-in-law, started Heads Together. This charity educates people about mental health issues and encourages people to seek help. It provides resources and assistance for people with mental health issues.

When he returned to school, Harry spent an extra year at Ludgrove to get his grades up before applying to secondary school (high school). The extra work paid off, and he began attending secondary school at Eton College in Berkshire in 1998.

While there, sixteen-year-old Harry got into trouble. Despite being under eighteen, the legal drinking age, he went out drinking with friends. He also tried marijuana, an illegal drug in the United Kingdom. His bad behavior made headlines, and reporters called him the Party Prince. After he admitted his offenses to his father, Charles made him visit a South London drug clinic. Harry got an up-close look at the dangers that come from substance use.

Harry's friends helped him cope with the loss of his mother.

After that, Harry started acting more responsibly. He joined the Combined Cadet Force, a military-themed youth organization. It was a good introduction to the armed forces. The organization promoted him to cadet officer. He led forty-eight cadets in the prestigious annual tattoo (a military demonstration).

At Eton he studied advanced-level courses in art, art history, and geography. However, Harry didn't want to go to a university after graduating from Eton in 2003. Instead, he wanted to start a military career. He got into the Royal Military Academy Sandhurst, the British Army's officer training center.

But before heading to Sandhurst, Harry took what's called a gap year. Many European students take a gap year, or a year to travel the world before continuing school or beginning a career. Harry focused his gap year on three different work experiences in three different places: Australia, Argentina, and Africa. In Australia he worked at a cattle station, training as a cowboy. In Argentina he worked on a polo farm, raising and training ponies to play polo. Polo is a sport where players ride on horses and use a long-handled mallet to knock a ball into a goal.

In Africa Harry went to Lesotho to work at an orphanage for children with AIDS (a disease caused by the HIV virus, which attacks the immune system). Harry built rooms, put up fences, and painted walls. He also played with the children and taught them English. Harry's mother had devoted much of her time to bringing awareness to AIDS, so Harry wanted to continue

Harry and a little boy named Mutsu Potsane plant a peach tree together at an orphanage in Lesotho in 2004.

her work. Harry produced a documentary called *The Forgotten Kingdom: Prince Harry in Lesotho* and raised close to $2 million from the film for the British Red Cross Lesotho Fund.

Military Man

After returning to England from his gap year, Harry attended his father's wedding to Camilla Parker Bowles on April 9, 2005. Charles and Camilla had known each other for many years. When asked about the wedding,

Harry (*center*) learned military discipline at the Royal Military Academy Sandhurst in Camberley, England.

Harry said, "She's always been very close to me and William. . . . She's a wonderful woman and she's made our father very, very happy, which is the most important thing."

The following month, Harry began his training at the Royal Military Academy Sandhurst. He graduated a year later and moved into his first army barracks, a building that houses soldiers. He started a special training course in 2006 at Bovington Camp, a British military base in Dorset. He was training to qualify as an armored reconnaissance troop leader, a person who commands soldiers and armored vehicles during exercises and training. He also joined a squadron that was due to deploy to Iraq in 2007.

However, after the deployment plans became public, British military leaders decided not to deploy Harry's unit. They thought Harry's presence would make the unit a target, endangering his life and the lives of other soldiers.

Harry was bitterly disappointed that he could not serve his country in Iraq. Later that year, British media outlets agreed not to publish details about Harry's next deployment. This would allow the prince's location to remain a secret from enemy forces. In December 2007, Harry began serving a tour of duty in Afghanistan. His service was part of a NATO-led effort to remove terrorists from power in the country.

In February 2008, just two months after his deployment, news outlets broke the story that Harry was in Afghanistan, and he was recalled from duty. "I felt very resentful. . . . I felt as though I was really achieving something. I have a deep understanding of all sorts of people from different backgrounds

Harry says the time he spent in Afghanistan inspired him to help injured soldiers. He later launched the Invictus Games, a worldwide athletic competition for wounded military veterans.

William and Kate married at Westminster Abbey on April 19, 2011. Harry is seen here following the couple out of the famous London church after the ceremony.

and felt I was part of a team. I wasn't a Prince, I was just Harry."

Upon his return to England, Harry decided to train as an Apache helicopter pilot. The position would make it harder for the press to track him on the battlefield, while still allowing him to serve on the front lines. Harry trained with the Army Air Corps starting in 2009.

Harry took a brief break from training in 2011 for William's wedding to Catherine (Kate) Middleton. Harry served as best man in the wedding. As his date, he brought his on-again off-again girlfriend Chelsea Davy. The gala event included the elaborate and historical ceremonies that are part of a royal wedding. Harry was delighted to welcome Kate into the family. He said, "I get a sister, which I have always wanted."

After the wedding, Harry returned to his Apache helicopter training. By 2012 he was ready to use his new skills on a second tour of duty. He was deployed to Afghanistan in September 2012 for a twenty-week tour.

Harry served as a copilot gunner in Helmand Province, where there was heavy Taliban fighting. He flew on several combat missions and helped to

The British Army in Iraq and Afghanistan

The United Kingdom became involved in the war in Afghanistan after terrorists attacked the United States on September 11, 2001. In 2002 the United Kingdom joined the NATO-led operations for peacekeeping and maintaining security in the area. In 2003 British troops went into Iraq to support the US-led invasion and remove Iraq's dictator, Saddam Hussein, from power.

Since then, British and US troops have worked to restore order in these countries. Over the years, both countries have withdrawn many troops in these regions. But militant and terrorist groups such as ISIS still fight for control of the region. Troops from the United States, the United Kingdom, and other countries continue to fight in these war-torn countries when security threats arise.

In 2013 Harry passed a test to become an Apache helicopter commander. That meant he could take command of the vehicle on missions.

deter Taliban soldiers away from British troops on the ground. He was proud of the work the British Army was doing in Afghanistan, helping to build up the Afghan National Army.

After ten years serving in the British Army, Harry decided to end his military career in 2015. He loved the job, in part, because it got him out of the limelight as a member of the royal family. But it also taught him to work hard and support his fellow soldiers. That sense of friendship and loyalty was invaluable. Harry continues to speak highly of his time in the military and recommends service for any young person.

He focused on charity work after leaving the military. Harry always felt a connection with the people in Africa,

Harry works to protect the people and environment of Africa. He attended the opening of the Mamohato Children's Centre in Lesotho in 2015. The organization helps vulnerable young people in the country.

especially in Lesotho. Harry has often said he feels more himself in Africa than anywhere else. "I have this intense sense of complete relaxation and normality here. To not get recognized, to lose myself in the bush with . . . people [dedicated to conservation] with no ulterior motives, no agendas, who would sacrifice everything for the betterment of nature."

Harry uses his position in the royal family to direct attention to the causes he cares about most. He continues to work with children, particularly those with HIV and AIDS. He's also promoting conservation that saves wildlife in Africa.

Harry had a new focus for his future. Free of his military duties, he had more time to spend with his family too. William and Kate had two young children, George and Charlotte. Harry adored his nephew and niece, and he was beginning to consider starting a family of his own one day. But first, he had to meet the right person.

Harry stands behind Kate and William in 2016. William kneels beside George as Kate holds Charlotte.

Young Meghan

Rachel Meghan Markle was born in Los Angeles, California, on August 4, 1981. Her mother, Doria, is a social worker and yoga instructor. Her father, Tom, works in the television industry as a lighting and photography director. Despite having the first name Rachel, everyone calls her Meghan.

The family lived in Hollywood, and she attended

preschool at the Hollywood Little Red School House. Her father picked her up after school and often took her to the set of the sitcom he worked on, *Married with Children*. She spent time with the cast and guest stars. It was her introduction to the entertainment industry.

Her racial identity has shaped Meghan's life in many ways. Meghan is biracial: her mother is African American, and her father is Caucasian. She didn't look much like her mother, so some people assumed Doria wasn't Meghan's mom. At that time, biracial families were less accepted by some members of American society. But Meghan's parents tried to make her feel that their family wasn't any different from other families. When she was seven years old, Meghan asked for a set of Barbie dolls. She wanted a family set that included a mother, father, and two children. The dolls were sold as either all-white families or all-black families. But when Meghan opened her gift on Christmas morning, she found a set with a black mother and a white father. Her dad had bought both sets and created a family of dolls that looked like their family.

Meghan attended private Catholic schools, and as she got older, she had to deal with racial ignorance from teachers. When she was in seventh grade, Meghan and her classmates filled out a mandatory census form in class. She had to pick her race, but the boxes only included the choices of black, white, Hispanic, or Asian. She didn't know which box she was supposed to check, so she asked her teacher. The teacher told her to check

Meghan claps alongside her mother at the 2017 Invictus Games.

the box for white, because that was how she looked. But Meghan couldn't bring herself to do it. She thought it would hurt her mother's feelings if she didn't acknowledge her African American heritage too. Instead, Meghan left the boxes blank. She later told her father what had happened in school and her teacher's response to her question. Angry at the teacher's ignorance, her dad gave Meghan a piece of advice that has always stuck with her. He said, "If that happens again, you draw your own box."

Meghan caught the acting bug by starring in school plays at Immaculate Heart High School. She was in several productions at the all-girls school and in *Damn Yankees* at a neighboring school for boys. A former teacher, Christine Knudsen, remembers Meghan as someone who loved to sing and dance, and who had a lot of inner strength. Other teachers remember Meghan as a good student who had compassion for people in need, such as homeless people and former gang members.

After high school, Meghan went to Northwestern University in Illinois. She loved acting, but Meghan was conflicted about choosing a major. "I knew I wanted to do acting, but I hated the idea of being this cliché—a girl from L.A. who decides to be an actress," Meghan said. "I wanted more than that, and I had always loved politics, so I ended up changing my major completely, and double-majoring in theater and international relations."

Meghan is passionate about social issues around the world and has spoken out on race and women's rights. In her junior year, she applied for an internship at the US Embassy in Buenos Aires, Argentina. She worked for several months at the embassy. She immersed herself in her work and in the Spanish language so she could better communicate with Argentinians. While she was there, Argentina's economy was doing poorly, and many people didn't have jobs. The US secretary of the treasury visited Argentina to work with their government, and Meghan traveled around the city in his motorcade. It was a very exciting time, and Meghan was sure she would end up having a career in politics.

When she returned home, however, a friend put Meghan in touch with an entertainment manager. He saw a student film that Meghan had performed in and took her on as a client. In 2002 Meghan appeared in her first television role. She was in the background on the afternoon soap opera *General Hospital*. It wasn't much of a role, but she hoped it would lead to an acting career.

Making It in Hollywood

Meghan graduated from Northwestern University in 2003. Then she returned home to Los Angeles and started looking for work as an actor. She had a few early successes: guest roles on television shows like *Century City* and *CSI: NY*. But it wasn't enough to make a career.

To support herself, Meghan used her artistic handwriting skills as a freelance calligrapher. She first honed her penmanship skills at the Catholic schools she had attended. In between auditions, she would handwrite note cards for her clients. Meghan created the invitations for musician Robin Thicke and actor Paula Patton's wedding. She also wrote holiday notes for the luxury fashion line Dolce & Gabbana.

Her calligraphy work helped pay the bills, but Meghan struggled to find acting roles. She did a few modeling gigs and regularly appeared on the game show *Deal or No Deal*. Part of her difficulty landing work came from her biracial identity. She looked ethnically ambiguous: not quite white and not quite black. She went to auditions where they were casting for Latina, African American, or Caucasian roles. But despite continuing to get invitations to auditions, she failed to land the parts. "I wasn't black enough for the black roles and I wasn't white enough for the white ones, leaving me somewhere in the middle as the ethnic chameleon who couldn't book a job," she stated.

That changed in 2011 when Meghan landed her first big role on the USA Network television show *Suits*. The

Meghan (*top*) appeared on *Deal or No Deal* from 2006 to 2007.

producers wanted to cast a "dream girl" role. Typically, in the acting world, a "dream girl" character was a white woman with blond hair and blue eyes, but the *Suits* producers didn't specify a race for their character. They were just looking to fill the role of a beautiful and confident woman who was an expert in law. After her audition, the producers chose Meghan for the role. Meghan says the role is "the Goldilocks of my acting career—where finally I was just right." It was a long way from her days of working on a game show or as a background character on a soap opera.

Suits is a legal drama set in a New York City law firm. Meghan played Rachel Zane, who started as a paralegal

Meghan left *Suits* in 2018 after seven seasons on the show.

in the show. Over the course of the show, Zane attended Columbia University and achieved her dream of becoming an attorney.

Meghan's character on *Suits* was also biracial. At the end of the second season of the show, the producers cast Rachel's father as an African American man, played by Wendell Pierce. Many viewers did not realize that Meghan and the character she played were biracial, and the casting of her father surprised viewers. Some said offensive things about Meghan after they found out she was biracial. Their reactions brought public attention to the racism that many people of color face in the United States.

Meghan has used her platform as a television star to speak out on issues that are important to her. "The moment *Suits* became successful and I realized people (especially young girls) were listening to what I had to say, I knew I needed to be saying something of value," Meghan said. She has championed gender equality, clean-water campaigns, and pet adoption. In 2015 Meghan spoke at a United Nations (UN) conference on International Women's Day. Later, she became the UN Women's Advocate for Political Participation and Leadership. As part of this role, Meghan traveled to Rwanda, where she met with women leaders in the government and discussed issues regarding the country's refugee camps.

Though she found it difficult to move between Hollywood fantasy and real-life conditions in developing countries, Meghan was dedicated to her humanitarian work. She felt that her fame gave her a responsibility to help those in need.

In her personal life, Meghan had some difficulties with romance. She married film producer Trevor Engelson in 2011, but the marriage did not last. After just two years, they divorced. Meghan was still looking for the right man.

A Whirlwind Romance

In June 2016, Meghan's life would change in an unexpected way. That's when she met Harry on a blind date set up by a mutual friend. Despite both Harry and Meghan being in the public eye, they didn't know much about each other before the date. Since she was from the United States, Meghan didn't know as much about the royal family as most people in the United Kingdom did. Though she had certainly heard of Harry before they met, Meghan just wanted to know if he was nice. Harry had not seen *Suits* before he met Meghan.

During their date, Meghan and Harry hit it off immediately. It was the beginning of their whirlwind romance. Harry asked Meghan for another date the following day. During this date, Harry persuaded Meghan to travel to Africa with him. While there, they camped out under the stars. The trip gave them time to get to know each other out of the spotlight.

Just four months after their first date, on October 31, 2016, news got out that Harry and Meghan were in a relationship. The tabloids ran wild as reporters speculated about the romance. Reporters and photographers lurked outside her mother's house, and they even tried to gain illegal entry to Meghan's home. The media bombarded nearly every one of Meghan's friends, coworkers, or loved ones with interview requests.

The tabloids also wrote about Meghan's biracial identity in a negative way. The mixture of harassment, sexism, and racism in the articles was alarming to the couple. On November 8, Harry released a public statement confirming the relationship and asking the press to stop harassing Meghan and printing negative articles about her. Harry was all too familiar with tabloid culture, but Meghan, despite being an actor, was completely

Meghan and Harry have fun during an event at the 2017 Invictus Games in Toronto, Canada. Harry proposed to Meghan a few days later.

unprepared for the onslaught of media coverage. Harry wanted to protect her from it if he could.

The couple kept their relationship private as much as possible. With Meghan's filming schedule and Harry's charity work, the couple had to maintain a long-distance relationship. They split their time between London and Toronto, where *Suits* was filmed. They frequently traveled to spend time together outside of the public eye. Together, they visited Botswana, Norway, and Jamaica. Harry introduced Meghan to members of his family, including Queen Elizabeth. Meghan said, "It's incredible to be able to meet her through his lens, not just with his honor and respect for her as the monarch, but the love that he has for her as his grandmother. She's an incredible woman."

After dating for a little more than a year, Harry knew he had found the woman he wanted to marry. In early November 2017, the couple was roasting a chicken for dinner and having a quiet night in Nottingham Cottage, their small home on the grounds of Kensington Palace. Harry got down on one knee and caught Meghan by surprise by proposing. Excited and nervous, Meghan tried to say yes before Harry had even finished the proposal. The couple enjoyed a quiet engagement for a few weeks before announcing the news to the public. They released their official announcement on November 27, 2017.

Both families were thrilled about the engagement. Meghan's parents said, "We are incredibly happy for Meghan and Harry. Our daughter has always been a kind and loving person. To see her union with Harry, who shares the same qualities, is a source of great joy for us as parents." William, Kate, Prince Charles, and Queen Elizabeth also shared their warm wishes for the couple.

Looking to the Future

The couple announced that the wedding would take place on May 19, 2018. They would wed at St. George's Chapel at Windsor Castle in England. It was a beautiful sunny day as guests arrived at the chapel for the big event. Since it was a private wedding and not a state event,

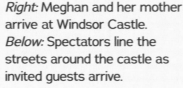

Right: Meghan and her mother arrive at Windsor Castle.
Below: Spectators line the streets around the castle as invited guests arrive.

the couple did not invite political leaders. Instead, the six hundred guests were a diverse mix of royal family, friends, and celebrities. Some of the famous guests included Oprah Winfrey, Elton John, Serena Williams, and George and Amal Clooney. The royal couple also invited twelve hundred other people to the Windsor Castle grounds in recognition of charity work these chosen guests had done in their communities.

All eyes were on Meghan as she climbed the steps of Windsor Castle. She wore a simple and elegant white gown and a long lace-trimmed veil. Her father could

Meghan walks down the aisle during the ceremony at St. George's Chapel.

attend the wedding for health reasons, so Meghan walked by herself halfway down the aisle. Then Harry's father, Prince Charles, joined Meghan and walked with her to the front of the chapel where Harry was waiting in his military uniform. The ceremony was infused with several American elements. The Reverend Michael Curry, the first African American head of the Episcopal Church, delivered an emotional and stirring sermon. He spoke about the power of love to change the world. Following his sermon was a moving version of the 1961 American hit song "Stand by Me," sung by a gospel group called the Kingdom Choir. Following the ceremony, guests attended a luncheon hosted by the queen. Later, two hundred guests attended a dinner reception hosted by Prince Charles, which was capped off by a colorful fireworks display.

The queen gave the couple the official royal titles of Duke and Duchess of Sussex. Three days after the wedding, Harry and Meghan performed their first royal duties as a married couple at a ceremony celebrating Prince Charles's seventieth birthday. They are looking forward to a lifetime of serving in the royal family and supporting the charities and organizations that they both care deeply about. Through their whirlwind romance and magnificent royal wedding, the couple has become an adored addition to the British royal family.

Meghan and Harry are all smiles after the ceremony at Windsor Castle.

IMPORTANT DATES

1981   Prince Charles and Princess Diana are married at St. Paul's Cathedral in London. Meghan Markle is born on August 4.

1984   Prince Harry is born on September 15.

1996   Charles and Diana are divorced.

1997   After a holiday with William and Harry, Diana dies in a car crash.

2002   Meghan is cast in her first television show, *General Hospital.*

2003   Meghan graduates from Northwestern University. Harry graduates from Eton College.

2005   Harry begins his training at the Royal Military Academy Sandhurst.

2006   Harry starts a special training course at Bovington Camp.

2007	Harry begins duty in Afghanistan.
2009	Harry begins training as an Apache helicopter pilot in the Army Air Corps.
2011	Meghan appears as a leading character on the television show *Suits*. She marries film producer Trevor Engelson.
2012	Harry begins his second tour of duty in Afghanistan.
2013	Meghan divorces Trevor Engelson.
2015	Harry ends his official military duties.
2017	Harry and Meghan announce their engagement on November 27.
2018	The royal wedding takes place on May 19 at St. George's Chapel at Windsor Castle.

SOURCE NOTES

7   Caroline Hallemann, "Meghan Markle's Engagement Ring Is Absolutely Stunning," *Town and Country*, January 9, 2018, http://www.townandcountrymag.com/society/tradition /a13090749/meghan-markle-engagement-ring/.

17–18   Britt Stephens, "30 Sweet, Heartbreaking Things William and Harry Have Said about Princess Diana," PopSugar, September 27, 2017, https://www.popsugar.com/celebrity/Prince-William -Prince-Harry-Quotes-About-Princess-Diana-43341113.

18   Diana Pearl, "Prince Harry's Most Revealing Quotes about His Near Breakdown: 'I Refused to Ever Think about My Mom,'" *People*, April 17, 2017, http://people.com/royals/prince-harrys -most-revealing-quotes-about-his-near-breakdown-i-refused-to -ever-think-about-my-mom/.

18   Pearl.

22   "Prince Harry Biography," Biography.com, March 19, 2018, https://www.biography.com/people/prince-harry-9542035.

23–24   Diana Pearl, "14 Times Prince Harry Got Seriously Raw," *People*, June 28, 2017, http://people.com/royals/14-times-prince-harry -got-seriously-raw/he-felt-most-at-home-in-the-army-and -resented-the-journalist-who-outed-his-afghanistan-service.

24   "Read Royal Reactions to William and Kate's Engagement," PopSugar, November 22, 2010, https://www.popsugar.com.au /celebrity/photo-gallery/12170531/image/12170528/Prince -Charles.

27   Morgan Evans, "Prince Harry Opens Up about the One Place He Feels Most at Home," *Harper's Bazaar*, January 3, 2017, http:// www.harpersbazaar.com/culture/features/news/a19694/prince -harry-town-and-country-interview-africa/.

30   Meghan Markle, "Meghan Markle: I'm More Than an 'Other,'" *Elle* (UK), December 12, 2016, http://www.elleuk.com/life-and -culture/news/a26855/more-than-an-other/.

31   Maura Brannigan, "Exclusive: Q&A with *Suits*' Meghan Markle," *Marie Claire*, June 5, 2013, http://www.marieclaire.com/celebrity /news/a7733/meghan-markle-interview/.

32   Markle, "I'm More."

33   Markle.

34–35   Meghan Markle, "Meghan Markle for ELLE: 'With Fame Comes Opportunity, but Also a Responsibility,'" *Elle* (UK), November 8, 2016, http://www.elleuk.com/life-and-culture/elle-voices/articles /a32612/meghan-markle-fame-comes-responsibility.

37–38   Morgan Evans, "A Definitive History of Prince Harry and Meghan Markle's Royal Relationship," *Town and Country*, January 24, 2018, http://www.townandcountrymag.com/society /a9664508/prince-harry-meghan-markle-relationship/.

38   Katie Frost, "Prince Harry and Meghan Markle Are Engaged!," *Town and Country*, November 27, 2017, https://www .townandcountrymag.com/society/tradition/a12198435 /prince-harry-meghan-markle-engaged/.

SELECTED BIBLIOGRAPHY

Junor, Penny. *Prince Harry: Brother, Soldier, Son.* New York: Grand Central, 2014.

Kashner, Sam. "Meghan Markle: Wild about Harry!" *Vanity Fair*, September 6, 2017. https://www.vanityfair.com/style/2017/09 /meghan-markle-cover-story.

Larcombe, Duncan. *Prince Harry: The Inside Story.* New York: HarperCollins, 2017.

Morton, Andrew. *Diana: Her True Story—in Her Own Words.* New York: Simon & Schuster, 2017.

Nicholl, Katie. *Harry: Life, Loss, and Love.* New York: Hachette, 2018.

——. *William and Harry: Behind the Palace Walls.* New York: Hachette, 2010.

Simmons, Simone, and Ingrid Seward. *Diana: The Last Word.* New York: St. Martin's, 2005.

Wilson, A. N. *The Queen.* New York: Atlantic Books, 2016.

FURTHER READING

BOOKS

Doeden, Matt. *Prince William & Kate: A Royal Romance*. Minneapolis: Lerner Publications, 2012. Learn more about Britain's royal family and William and Kate's wedding in 2011.

Novis, Constance, and Helen Fewster, eds. *Queen Elizabeth II and the Royal Family*. New York: DK, 2015. Read about the history of British royalty, from the country's first monarchs to Queen Elizabeth II.

Sadat, Halima. *Harry and Meghan: A Royal Engagement*. London: Pavilion, 2018. Read this book to learn more about Meghan, Harry, and their engagement.

WEBSITES

How Royalty Works
https://history.howstuffworks.com/historical-figures/royalty.htm
Learn more about royalty around the world, how royal families come into power, and what rules govern the passing of that power from generation to generation.

Meghan Markle Biography
https://www.biography.com/people/meghan-markle-013117
Read about Meghan, and watch a video about the former actor's life. The page also links to the biographies of other royals, including Prince Harry.

Prince Harry
http://www.royal.gov.uk/TheCurrentRoyalFamily/PrinceHarry/PrinceHarry.aspx
This is Prince Harry's page on the official website of the British monarchy. It includes a biography, photo gallery, and links to other members of the royal family.

INDEX